THE CHRISTMAS WONDER

A BWWM Holiday Mènage Romance

A LANGDALE CHRISTMAS
BOOK IV

PEYTON BANKS

"In dreams and in love there are no impossibilities."

— JANOS ARANY

Copyright © 2024 by Peyton Banks

Editor: Five Hive Media

Cover Design by Peyton Banks

This is a work of fiction. Names, characters, organizations, businesses, events, and incidents are a figment of the author's imagination and are used fictitiously. Any similarities to real people, businesses, locations, history, and events are a coincidence.

All rights reserved.

No part of this publication may be reproduced, distributed, or transmitted in any form or by any means, including photocopying, recording, or other electronic or mechanical methods, without the prior written permission of the publisher.

Information about the copyright permissions of the stock photos used can be provided upon request.

 Created with Vellum

BLURB

Santa was paying close attention to his list this year...

Elementary school teacher Skye Roberts wondered when it would be her turn to fall in love. Christmas was fast approaching, and she had hoped Santa would have sent her one true love by now. But the only thing she had received was a request from her boss to orient the new physical education teacher.

Ward Snider recently moved to Langdale to get his dream job. He hadn't hesitated to leave the big city to relocate to a small town. He was ready for a slower pace, and it helped that his best friend worked at the same school. Only Fin hadn't mentioned the beautiful woman who would be showing him the ropes.

Fin Milkowski hadn't hesitated to help Ward obtain a job when the previous gym teacher suddenly retired. They had become close in college and did everything together. Fin and Ward wanted Skye and had no problem sharing her.

Helping the new hire started off innocently enough. Only Skye was not prepared for two men giving her the attention she had desired. Ward and Fin were a temptation she couldn't resist. When a winter storm forced them to spend the night together, Skye realized she wouldn't have to choose between them. This holiday, Santa had delivered double the gifts.

The Christmas Wonder is a steamy, BWWM menage holiday romance. For readers who love sexy, small-town MFM romance, this is for you. This short novella is reserved for mature readers only.

1

"Of course the weatherman is calling for more snow," Skye Roberts muttered. She placed her cellphone down on her desk and sighed. This was Langdale. Why *wouldn't* more snow be on the way? For some strange reason Mother Nature always had it out for their small town during the winter. The last few Decembers had record amounts of snow, and this year was headed in the same direction.

Whoever pissed Mother Nature off had better go apologize to the woman.

Skye glanced out the window of her classroom and stared out at the winter wonderland that waited for her. Today was the last day of classes before the holiday break, and she didn't know who was more excited to be off, her or the kids.

Skye loved teaching her third grade kiddos. When she was a little girl, all she'd ever wanted to be was a schoolteacher. She honestly couldn't see herself doing anything else. Helping to mold the young minds of potential future leaders was a rewarding job, but sometimes even the teacher needed a break.

This time of year was her favorite, and Skye was looking forward to the next two weeks. Not that she had much planned, but the fact that she wouldn't have to get dressed if she didn't want too was enough to get her excited. She had a few good books waiting for her, and of course she planned to go over to her parent's house for the holiday. Skye wasn't going to let a little snow make her miss out on her mother's cooking.

Last year there was a winter storm that almost ruined dinner, but Alma Roberts had been ready. Hopefully this year there would be no Christmas storm trying to ruin the holiday.

Skye settled back in her chair and

glanced down at the sticky note on her computer screen. A sigh escaped her. A week and a half ago, she'd received a notification from her boss that she would be needed to orient the new teacher.

Mr. Loeb, the dedicated physical education teacher who had worked for the Langdale school system for thirty-five years decided to up and retire without giving anyone notice. To say that it was a shock to everyone was an understatement. There had been rumors that he was thinking of retiring at the end of the school year, but apparently he had changed his mind. Luckily, they were only without a P.E. teacher for a few weeks before Mr. Snider was hired.

Ward Snider.

Skye couldn't help but sigh again. She, and every woman with a pulse who worked at the school, had noticed him. How could they not when he walked in the school. He was tall, muscular, had dark blond hair, and the weirdest shade of gray eyes Skye had ever seen. The rumor mill was hot with the news that not only was he new to town, but he was single.

And she got to be in charge of his orientation. She had planned to show him around and then help him acclimate to Langdale's grading system. She'd answer any questions he might have, and hopefully be able to keep from saying anything embarrassing. Skye glanced down at her watch. This was her planning period and she had a little time on her hands. On a whim, she decided that she would go check on the new gym teacher and see if he needed anything from her.

Work related things... obviously.

What she wouldn't give for him to need her in another way.

Skye snorted at the thought.

That was a daydream for when she wasn't sitting in her third grade classroom that had been decorated by her kids for the holidays. She pushed back from her desk and stretched. Ward was a little hard to figure out. He seemed like a nice guy, and so far all the kids liked him. Skye was usually good at reading people, but with him, it was like he'd thrown up a shield.

Skye glanced down at her jeans and the ugly Christmas sweater she had worn. The theme for the last day of school before Christmas was her favorite. There was a school-wide Ugly Sweater Contest going on, and the winner would be drawn at the end of the day. Skye was hoping to win this year. The Java Hut gift card was as good as hers— No one's sweater was as ugly as the one she'd picked out.

She made her way out of her room and locked her classroom door behind her. A small smile appeared on her lips as she walked down the halls toward the gym. The school was a pretty nice sized building and it would take her about five to seven minutes to get to the gymnasium.

It was certainly Christmas time. Throughout the school there were Christmas trees, garland, lights, stars, and snowmen decorating the halls. The kids and teachers took great pride in making sure the school was very festive. Holiday music could be heard floating from quite a few classrooms.

Skye hummed the catchy tune of Jingle Bells as she walked. She would admit she was the kind of person who started playing Christmas music right after Halloween. Most people would think she was crazy, but dammit, she loved this time of year. She just wished she would have one Christmas where Santa would finally bring her the only thing she had on her wish list.

A life partner.

Why hasn't she been as lucky as others and found a soul mate? Skye was tired of going home to an empty house. She would love to have someone to cook for and snuggle up on the couch with during these cold winter days and watch old movies while a fire crackled in the hearth.

Where was her special someone?

Was he even out there?

Apparently, Santa just hadn't seen fit to put a man underneath her tree or in the stockings she'd hung on her mantle.

Skye turned the corner near the gymnasium and felt a flutter in her belly. It was the same feeling she got whenever she was around Ward. That man's intense stare always had her stumbling over her words when she was near him.

"Skye," a deep voice called out to her. She paused and felt that sensation increase. It wasn't Ward's voice.

It was Fin's.

She glanced over her shoulder and tried

not to make it obvious as she looked Fin Milkowski up and down as he leaned in the doorway of his classroom. The seventh grade science teacher was also on the list of single hot male teachers the women of the school gossiped about.

Skye would admit she loved chilling in the teacher's lounge where she could catch up on all the latest news. She didn't have much going on with her life, so she had to live vicariously through others.

Fin was recently single. He and his longtime girlfriend had only just broken up. No one seemed to know what had happened, but Skye was dying to know. How was a guy like Fin not married with a ton of kids?

She met his stare and inhaled sharply. There was something about Fin that made Skye's heart race. His dark brown hair, and hazel eyes which were always hidden behind his dark rimmed glasses unlocked a kink she hadn't even realized she had.

The nerdy guy kink.

"Hey, Fin," she murmured. She reached up and nervously tucked her hair behind her ear. Skye had known Fin for a few years. Even though he taught middle grade, she still knew most of the teachers. He pushed his glasses up higher on the bridge of his nose and smiled at her. It was a simple move, but it had her wanting to see what he would look like without the frames on his face or better yet, what he'd look like braced over her. Skye blinked and pushed that thought out of her head. "What's up?"

"Nothing. You just had a weird look on your face. I called your name twice, but you didn't hear me." He grinned at her and tossed her a wink. Her cheeks warmed with embarrassment—had she really been that zoned out?. How had she not heard someone call her name? She was too focused on going to see Ward.

"Where are you off to?" he asked.

"I was going to check in with Ward. Make sure he's doing okay," she said. A few middle schoolers were walking down the hall and she moved toward Fin to allow them to pass. The scent of his cologne filled her senses and. she breathed it in and had to fight the urge to close her eyes and revel in it. He would certainly think she was a perv or something weird if she did that. Why was it whenever she was around an attractive guy she acted like a klutz? Why couldn't she be cool and sophisticated like Sheila, the fifth grade teacher. Even though Sheila was a bitch, she always looked good and Skye was sure that she never made a fool of herself in front of anyone. "I'm sure Ward is doing fine. He's been at this for a while." Fin folded his arms across his chest. She took notice of how the material of his button down shirt stretched out around his torso. She bit her lip and dragged her eyes away from his exposed forearms. "He always did pick things up quickly."

"Ward did mention you two were friends," Skye said. She cleared her throat as she thought of a conversation they'd had when Ward had first arrived at the school. Their casual conversation had led her to asking how he had found Langdale. Their small town certainly couldn't compete with the big school districts in the major cities.

"Yeah. We met in college our sophomore year. Been close friends ever since," Fin said.

"Mr. Milkowski? I have a question," a young male voice called out from somewhere in the room behind them.

"Looks like I have to get back to work.

They're taking a quiz." Fin smiled at her and Skye felt butterflies ramp up in her stomach again. He pushed his glasses up on his nose again. "Tell Ward I'll stop by soon."

"Okay." She smiled and gave him a little wave as he spun on his heel and went back into the classroom. She leaned forward and peeked inside and saw the kids spread out at their lab stations working silently.

"What's up, Jake?" Fin asked as he went over to a slender kid with auburn hair.

Skye backed away and continued down the hallway toward the gym. She couldn't shake the grin off her lips. The kids loved Fin's class. She always had some of her older kids stopping in to visit her and they always mentioned how fun Mr. Milkowski's science classes were.

Skye finally arrived at the gymnasium and noticed that there were no kids. A silent gymnasium? It was strange. She wiped her suddenly sweaty palms on her jeans and headed in.

She was just here to do her job and check in on the new teacher.

2

Ward leaned back in his chair and stared at the computer screen. This system was different from the one he was used to at his old school. He had a free period and was trying to enter grades for the students from that morning's classes.

The program wasn't a hard one, it just had extra steps that he had to remember. He'd written down a few notes for when he would meet with Skye.

Ward thought of the third grade teacher who had been assigned to orient him. She was breathtakingly beautiful. Her warm brown skin, big brown eyes, and curvy hips definitely called to him. He especially liked how she appeared to be shy and skittish around him when they were alone.

He'd seen her with her kids and the woman commanded respect from them without being overbearing. On his first day, her class had started to get a little rowdy and it only took one word from her to make them settle down immediately.

His attention had been piqued then.

With his recent move from Chicago to Langdale, he hadn't had a chance to really get out and meet most of the townsfolk. Since the previous P.E. teacher had retired with no notice, he'd started work right away. He hadn't minded. Ward loved to stay busy, and with the winter break coming up, he'd take the time off to finish unpacking and explore the town more fully.

After teaching in Chicago public schools for years, he needed a change. Ward had loved teaching the children of his district and he had met some great kids over the years, but they faced certain challenges that he as a teacher was unable to meet and it pained him. Budget cuts were always coming and that made it extremely hard to do his job. The teachers had to fight to get the necessary tools they needed to educate the kids and he was tired of battling for necessities.

Leaving his old school hadn't been an easy decision, but when an opportunity like this one came up, he just couldn't pass it up. A new start was what he needed, and he'd been close to his good friend, Fin. A grin appeared at the thought of the son of a bitch who got him to move to this small town.

He didn't have any problem with a small town. He had grown up in one just like Langdale, and it did remind him of home. A small town was definitely what he needed. So far, the sense of community had already reached him.

The day his moving truck showed up at his home, he'd already had three neighbors offering to come and help him unload. He'd accepted their help, and it made his and Fin's day go by much quicker. He'd already been invited to watch a few football games with a great group of guys from the street. He certainly hadn't received that type of reception when he'd moved into his apartment back in Chicago. He'd lived in the same building for eight years and only knew the older lady across the hall. Everyone else had pretty much stayed to themselves.

Ward stared at the computer screen again and felt the thing he was looking for was right in his face. He didn't want to ask Skye too many questions. Even though if he did that would mean he'd have her attention a little longer. He ran his hand along his face and remembered that he hadn't seen a wedding ring on her finger.

But that didn't mean much, nowadays. Not everyone got married. He'd have to ask Fin if Skye was single. Fin had said he'd known Skye for a few years.

"This will have to wait," he muttered. He glanced down at his notes and added another question to his long growing list for Skye. A knock echoed in the room and he glanced over his shoulder and saw her standing in the doorway.

How had she known he needed to speak with her? A grin spread wide on his face as he spun his chair around to face her. His office was small and cozy, and was located at the back of the gym with a large glass window to give him a full view of it. This was much more accommodating than his old gym, and the office was at least double the size of the one at his last school. He had already decorated his office to showcase his college days when he'd played football, his travels, and pictures of his family. The kids loved coming in to ask him questions to get to know him and ask about Chicago.

"How did you know you were on my mind?" he asked as she entered the office.

Skye's lips turned up into a soft smile. She reached up and tucked her thick hair behind her ear. He loved to see how she reacted to him. That shyness brought out something inside of him he was unfamiliar with. He wanted to see her unrestrained.

Beneath him.

He blinked and had to resist readjusting himself. His cock grew thick with the thought of seeing her naked curves. He was sure that smooth brown skin would be magnificent spread out on his bed with her dark hair against his crisp white pillows.

Fuck.

He needed to change his train of thought. They were at work for one, and any one of his kids could walk in. It wouldn't go over well that the gym teacher was aroused. With gray basketball shorts on, his erection would be noticeable. He tried to adjust the way he was sitting in his chair to hide anything that might be happening.

One of her perfectly arched eyebrows rose. "Is there something you need?" she asked. She pushed off the doorframe and entered the office. He breathed in her soft floral perfume and felt his cock pulse. He needed to think of something else to curb this desire for the petite third grade teacher. He didn't want to frighten her, or much worse, send her running off to human resources to report him for lewd behavior.

"Yeah, I'm just stuck on a few things." He cleared his throat and motioned to the computer screen. He had a little bit of time before his next class was to arrive. Discussing the kids and entering grades should kill this erection. Hopefully she wouldn't look down at his lap when she came near.

"What's going on?" Skye came closer and stood close to him. Her scent enveloped him and made him want to pull her down onto his lap.

Ward bit back a curse and reached for the list he'd made.

Skye's brown eyes slid down his torso and it was such a quick move that he didn't even know if she had realized she done it.

But those brown orbs landed on his lap and paused.

He bit back a curse. His fucking cock had a mind of its own and he gritted his teeth as it twitched.

What. The. Fuck.

Her eyes widened and her mouth dropped open slightly. He closed his eyes briefly and tried to erase the fantasy of those lips closing around his long thick length. He blinked and focused on her again. She was looking at the list in his hand now.

"Do you mind?" she asked as she took the notepad from him. He nodded, unable to find his voice.

Why was he having this type of reaction to her?

She scanned the list then smiled. "This is actually a common issue we all have. It's not just you. I've complained about this to the principal several times, but he told me that we'd have to make do. They can't afford another system upgrade. Here, let me show you."

Ward nodded and inhaled. He was going to have to stand to allow her to take the reins of his computer and chair. Skye took a step back to allow him to stand.

He was much taller than her, and her head barely reached his mid chest.

Her eyes landed on his fucking cock again and it took everything he had to not groan when her tongue came out and slid along her bottom lip.

He gritted his teeth and quickly scooted out of the way. Once she was seated and her back was to him, he reached down and adjusted himself.

"So I'm not crazy?" He finally found his voice. He cleared his throat and leaned down to watch her work. He braced his hand on the back of the chair while he looked over her shoulder.

"Nope. Not at all," she said brightly as though nothing had happened. "Lucky for you, it saved. But to export it into the actual grade book—Here's where you messed up." She typed in a few commands before glancing up at him. Her plump lips were shiny from whatever lip gloss she had on. Skye was a woman who embraced her natural beauty. He'd never seen her with tons of makeup on and that was how he preferred his women. He wanted to see the person beneath the makeup.

Skye was a natural beauty, and she took his breath away.

He cleared his throat. "You made that look so easy." The tension in the room was palpable, or was he just imagining it?

She had to feel it too.

Was that why she was always nervous around him?

He was a laid back guy and loved to laugh. Between him and Fin, he was the jokester and Fin was always the more serious of the two.

"Well, I've been using this system a lot longer than you." She smiled. She sat back in the chair and glanced around at his desk. "Looks like you're making yourself at home."

"Yeah. It goes over well with the kids. They like to go through the office and ask questions about everything."

"I'm not sure why. You're boring as fuck," a deep chuckle sounded from the door. Ward grinned at his friend who had snuck up on the two of them. Fin stood in the doorway with a smile on his face. His friend could be a dick sometimes, but Ward wouldn't have him any other way.

Skye's giggle floated through the room. He loved the sound of it.

"At least I'm the good-looking one," he countered. Fin walked in the room and they shared a quick brotherly hug before parting.

"You keep telling yourself that," Fin muttered. He focused his attention on Skye and motioned to Ward. "Don't let him take advantage of you. This motherfucker is lazy as hell."

"He's fine," she said with a hint of amusement in her voice. "Besides, I'm supposed to answer questions and help him out. Remember?" She spun the chair around and laughed again. Ward tossed her a wink and she did that thing she always did when she got nervous. She reached up and tucked her hair that was in place—behind her ear. He'd picked up on it the first day they'd met.

Was there something between Fin and Skye?

He didn't think so. His friend would have shared it with him. Especially since he and Lexi had broken up.

Fin had taken the split quite well, but it had been a long time coming and Ward had seen it from a mile away. Ward never thought Lexi was right for his friend. She was all about herself and drained as much as she could from his friend. He'd never liked her but accepted her only because Fin was into her. Thankfully his friend had finally come to his senses and left her before it was too late.

"All right, but if he gets out of hand, you let me know." Fin grinned. He slapped Ward on the shoulder. Fin gave his friend a playful shove away from him. They were as close as brothers and had done everything together. They'd gone on plenty of trips together—even though Lexi hadn't liked it.

What was wrong with a few guys going on a fishing trip? Or going on a diving trip down in Mexico?

He'd never understood how spending time with one's friends could cause a problem at home. It wasn't like they were doing anything crazy. Fin had never once cheated on her. He wasn't that type of guy. But hanging out with friends was an issue with her.

Again, Ward was happy that chick was gone.

"I'm sure we won't have any issues," Skye said.

"I'm always on my best behavior." Ward folded his arms across his chest. Now that his cock had decided to behave itself, he relaxed.

"That's what I'm afraid of," Fin muttered.

"You two are a mess," Skye chuckled.

"I don't have much time. I came down here to check on you and see if you still want to go out for a couple of drinks after work," Fin said. Ward hadn't forgotten his friend had texted him earlier about it. Fin had mentioned a great watering hole that had a few pool tables and it sounded like just the place he would love to hang out.

"Of course. But it's supposed to snow—

"I know you aren't scared of a little snow," Fin snorted.

Ward had heard they were supposed to be under a snowstorm watch for the weekend. He may have transferred from Chicago and was used to the cold, but even there he'd always heeded the warnings of the weatherman. Chicago's weather could be a bitch.

"People from Langdale don't let a little snow get them down," Skye stood and set her hands on her hips. Her sweater made Ward grin. She looked so cute. He'd seen a lot of the other teachers with their ugly sweaters on.

He glanced over and realized his friend wasn't participating in the contest, either.

"Well if you aren't worried, then I won't. Sure. A few drinks sound damn good to me." Ward nodded. He had a pick-up truck that could handle the snow. He just didn't know the town yet and had to see what the weather did here.

"How about you, Skye? Up for a few drinks after work?" Fin swung his focus to her. Ward's breath caught in his throat. This could be the opportunity he needed to get to know her a little bit and find out if there was something between these two.

"You sure? I wouldn't want to impose—"

"No way," Ward exclaimed. "You think I want to hang out with this dipshit alone? It would be fun. You should come." He leveled her with his gaze and smiled. Even though she had on that goddamn ugly sweater, it didn't hide her full breasts, her narrowed waist, or the flare of her hips in those jeans.

He glanced over at Fin and recognized the same look in his friend's eyes.

He wanted her too.

Interesting.

"Did you have plans?" Fin asked. Ward stiffened at the question.

What if she *did* have plans?

She shook her head and he relaxed.

Fin grinned and clapped his hands. "Then it looks like the three of us will be going out tonight after work."

Ward's gaze landed on Fin's. His friend was easy to read. There wasn't going to be a problem between the two of them when it came to Skye. They would allow her to choose.

3

Fin Milkowski was in good spirits. The holiday season was upon them, he was officially on break for the holiday, and his best friend was now living in the same town as him.

In addition to that, they had talked Skye Roberts into joining them for a few drinks after work.

The Little Pint was one of his favorite spots. The beer on tap was superb, the food was delicious, and the atmosphere was always what he needed after a long week of dealing with middle grade kids.

The Little Pint was decked out in Christmas decorations and Christmas music blared on the speakers. Everyone was definitely in the holiday spirit along with him. They were on their second round of drinks and had managed to talk Skye into playing pool. She had no experience, and Fin and Ward had offered to teach her.

Ward was up and was concentrating on his next shot. Fin rolled his eyes at his friend trying to showboat in front of Skye. They both had played plenty of pool in college and afterward. They were nowhere close to being professionals, but they could hang with the best pool players in any dive bar in the state.

"I didn't realize hitting a ball against another ball could be so hard," Skye giggled. She sipped on her drink and stood next to him. He had noticed that she avoided beer but loved a good cranberry and vodka. He could appreciate that. It was one of his mother's favorite go-to drinks.

Fin eyed her and felt the draw he'd always sensed when around her. He had ignored it before because he'd been in a long-term relationship with his ex-girlfriend, Lexi. But that shit hadn't worked out.

Ward had warned Fin a long time ago that he would need to watch out for Lexi.

His friend hadn't liked her, but he'd put up with her out of loyalty to Fin.

He should have listened. He had thought that it was just Ward being an ass and not liking her. Fin had always felt as though Lexi was taking advantage of him, but he had assumed he was doing what he was supposed to do in a relationship. But he should have known she wasn't the one when he had no desire to put a ring on her finger.

His mother had been hounding him about getting married and giving her some grandbabies, but when he tried to imagine Lexi being that person, he would feel sick to his stomach.

Lexi as a mother? Of his kids? That was never happening.

He didn't even think she liked children. Whenever she was around his kids at school for events, she would be distant with them.

That should have been a red flag.

Fin was a teacher who was around kids all day. Of course he grew attached to them and cared for them. He was human, and always tried to help the kids who were struggling. Science could be a hard subject for some kids, and Lexi never understood why he would stay late after school to go over questions with a student, or offer tutoring sessions online on Saturday mornings for those who were falling behind.

Fin loved what he did, and helping those who were craving knowledge gave him the best feeling in life. All of the men in his family were educators.

It was literally in his blood.

Fin's gaze landed on Skye and he found himself wanting to pursue her, but he'd seen the interest in his friend's eyes as well when they were in Ward's office. The two of them had never competed for a woman before. While he'd been in a committed relationship, Ward had stayed single—living the good life.

"It just takes practice. Tonight's your first time," he said. He pushed up his glasses that had slid down to the edge of his nose. She smiled and nodded. He was actually shocked that she had decided to come with them. He had anticipated having to ask her again, but he was pleasantly surprised she had said she'd come without too much hesitation.

Ward lined up his shot and hit the cue

ball, sending it to his striped target. The ball bounced around before it landed short of going into the pocket he'd called out.

"I'll be damned. That should have dropped," Ward scowled. He reached for his longneck and took a swig.

"That was still good. You got much closer than I did." Skye placed her glass down on the table and clapped. Ward glanced over at her and gave her his infamous crooked grin.

"Come on. It's your turn. I'll help you," Fin said. He downed the rest of his drink before setting the empty glass on the table. He snagged her cue and her hand to guide her over to where the white ball had landed. Fin had to admit her smaller hand felt damn good in his. He didn't miss the way Ward's gaze followed her.

How could he not? She was absolutely gorgeous. She had changed out of the ugly sweater she'd worn at work and had on a soft cream v-neck sweater that put her cleavage on display and those damn jeans showcased her wide hips and ample ass.

She'd caught the eye of quite a few men

that were in the bar, but Ward and Fin both warned them off with a hard glare.

Right now, she was with them.

Fin liked the sound of that. If there was anyone he had to share a woman with, it would be Ward.

"I'm horrible at this," she giggled.

"Fin is the best teacher around. He'll have you looking like a pro in no time," Ward teased. He leaned his hip along the table opposite from Fin and Skye. Fin pulled her in front of him and handed her the cue. He stepped forward, putting her back to his front. He bit back a groan at the feeling of her ass pressed against him.

He dropped his hand to her waist while he leaned down slightly placing his mouth near her ear. The place was loud and he wanted to make sure she heard his instructions.

"I got you," he said. Her body stiffened for a brief moment before she leaned into him. His cock took notice of her and twitched to life. His jeans were starting to feel way too damn small. She looked up at him over her shoulder with those bright brown eyes of hers. She smiled softly and he felt his heart skip a beat. "Now you'll need a firm grip along the cue. You won't break it."

She licked her lips and brought the cue up in her hand. She leaned over and positioned it along the table. This new position had Fin's eyes drawn to the span of her back and how perfect her ass looked in her jeans. He glanced up and saw Ward silently watching him while holding his beer. His friend didn't say a word before his gaze slipped back to the object of their desire.

Fin turned his attention back to Skye and leaned over with her.

A perfect fit.

His body molded along her curvy frame and Fin had to fight to concentrate and remember what he was doing. At the moment, all he wanted was to flip her over onto the table and slide her underneath him.

Instead, he helped her position the cue better and took aim at the solid orange ball. They were going to shoot for the corner pocket.

"Now before you strike the cue ball, you need to call out where you're going to send your target." His lips brushed her earlobe.

He didn't miss the shiver that went through her body.

"Okay," she breathed. She bit her bottom lip and pulled the stick back. Her eyes met his again.

"Go ahead. Call it," he murmured.

"Five, corner pocket," she announced.

"Good girl." He pressed a soft kiss to her shoulder and lifted up to allow her to take the shot. Ward's gaze was on him. He didn't have to look over at him to know. Skye sent her cue forward and the cracking sound cut through the air.

The white ball flew across the table and slammed into the solid orange ball. It slid along the table and found its target—the corner pocket.

"I did it!" Skye jumped up from her position, and her cue fell to the floor. She spun around with a wide grin on her face. Fin grinned back and opened his arms for her. She slammed into him and did a little dance. "Did you see that?"

"Of course. A little more practice and you'll be beating me," he chuckled. She pulled back but he wasn't ready to let her go just yet. He kept his arm around her waist

THE CHRISTMAS WONDER

and dropped a kiss to the top of her forehead. She leaned into him with her silly smile still in place. He was extremely pleased that she wasn't moving away from him. Ward sauntered over to them.

"I don't know about that," she breathed.

"I mean, he may know how to teach people how to play, that doesn't mean he knows how to win," Ward smirked. His eyes were locked on Skye. There was a feral glint in his gaze that mimicked what Fin felt in his chest.

"But did you see that shot?" Skye pointed to the pocket her ball had fallen into. Ward snagged her hand and tugged her forward. Fin missed her body next to his, but he didn't feel any jealousy watching Ward pull her to him.

Ward cupped her cheeks and leaned down and kissed her. Fin closed the gap and took her hand in his. She gripped his hand tight while she returned Ward's kiss. His friend lifted his head while still holding on to her face.

"You did good," Ward murmured. She leaned back against Fin and blinked. She glanced up at him over her shoulder. Her lips had already started to swell from Ward's kiss. Fin couldn't take his eyes off her pouty lips. She turned slightly to him and he brought her flush against him.

He lowered his head, and this time it was his turn to capture her lips with his. They were just as soft as he imagined they would be. Her mouth opened immediately allowing his tongue to sweep inside. Her fingers gripped his button down shirt tight. A moan slipped from her that had his cock growing even harder. He tore his lips from hers and opened his eyes. Hers were still closed as breaths came in pants.

Fin glanced up and found Ward behind her. She was sandwiched in between them and fit quite nicely, if he did say so. Ward inclined his head and that was all that needed to be said. They both wanted her and they would both have her. It wouldn't be the first time they had shared.

"Oh, my—um," Skye stuttered. She blinked and looked between Fin and Ward. He reached up and stroked the side of her face. He could tell that she was teetering on the edge of a dead panic. It was quite obvious by the way she kept looking at them.

"It's okay, Skye," Fin murmured.

"You don't have to choose," Ward said. Ward reached over and pushed her hair away from her eyes.

"I don't?" Her eyes widened. Fin shook his head and took her hand in his.

The music bumping through the speakers cut off suddenly. Fin stiffened and glanced over at the bar. He hadn't realized that the crowd had thinned out.

"Y'all still here may want to start heading out. The snow is getting mighty thick out there. They're already shutting down roads," Mike the bartender yelled out. Fin glanced over at Ward.

Well, fuck.

His friend might have had a good reason to be concerned about the weather.

Ward cocked an eyebrow at him as if to say, 'I told you so.'

"We should probably get out of here," Fin said.

"I'll go settle the bill. Grab your coats." Ward snagged their cues and hung them up on the wall before he headed over to the bar. The music came back on but this time the volume was cut way down. More of the patrons were leaving.

The weather must be getting bad out there if they actually listened to Mike.

"I don't know what came over me," Skye said as they walked over to the booth where they had left their jackets. He grabbed her coat and helped her slide it on. She threw her winter hat on top of her head. "I don't want to seem like a—

"Skye," he cut her off. He spun her around and helped her zip up her coat. He brought her close to him and tipped her chin up. Those brown eyes of hers were mesmerizing. "You don't have to choose. We'll figure it out."

"Seriously? You're both okay with what just happened?"

"She's not going to be able to drive her car. There's a shit ton of snow out there," Ward announced as he returned to the booth. He raked his fingers through his thick blond hair and shook his head. "We'd better leave. It really is coming down hard."

"What?" Skye spun around and glanced toward the door. "How am I going to get home?"

"Don't worry. We'll take you." Fin said. His truck could easily get through the deepest snow. They would leave her car in the bar's parking lot and he'd bring her back to get it once the storm blew over and the streets were cleared. He didn't even have to look outside to know her small sedan wouldn't make it.

"Okay," she said.

"Well, we had better leave now." Ward snagged his coat and threw it on. Fin shrugged into his coat and took Skye's hand in his.

"Let's go."

4

"Holy hell," Skye muttered.

She stood in the doorway of the Little Pint and stared at the mountains of snow that filled the parking lot. She'd worried for only a minute about going to a bar with her co-workers... but once she'd arrived, she'd had entirely too much fun. She couldn't remember the last time she'd laughed so hard. Skye didn't know what had come over her. Maybe it was the vodka in her system, or maybe she just wanted to live life a little, but she would definitely admit she had flirted with both Fin and Ward throughout the night.

She held their attention, and it felt damn good.

She felt wanted.

Sexy.

For the first time in a long time, she felt like a woman.

The alcohol did help loosen her up a bit. The guys had shared stories with her about their first time meeting in college, and all the trips they'd gone on together. It gave Skye a definite sense that they were truly the best of friends.

And she wanted both of them.

How could she choose?

As the night went on, she had just gone with the flow. Her favorite drink, cranberry and vodka, had hit the spot and given her a bit of courage.

But now staring at what the heavens had dumped on them, she was completely sober.

Everyone leaving the bar was trying to dig out their cars and trucks so they could leave. The way the snow was coming down, they were fighting an uphill battle. She tried to find her car in the mess and thanks to a snow drift, her car was barely visible.

"I'm parked over there," Fin pointed in the direction of a dark pickup. Steam rose from the exhaust and Skye guessed that he must have started it remotely.

"I'm right behind you," Ward announced.

"Let's get you in the truck." Fin said. He took one of her gloved hands in his while Ward grabbed the other. Her heart skipped a beat as she thought about what had happened inside the bar. Had she really been so brazen as to kiss both of them? Had that been the alcohol? Or was it a deep dark desire to be claimed by two sexy men?

The kisses were not just a peck on the lips, but full open mouth and tongue dueling with both of them. In public. Skye didn't think she would ever recover from such a moment. To be in between both of them had almost set her damn body ablaze.

When Ward had stalked toward her, the heat in his gaze had her frozen in place like a deer caught in headlights. The second his lips touched hers, she folded. Fin's solid body behind her helped keep her up.

She was thankful they had taken hold of her hands. Not only was the snow deep, but there was a layer of ice underneath it. She would have certainly gone down if it hadn't been for them holding on to her.

As they slowly made their way to Fin's truck, a deep chill settled into her bones in the short time it took them to walk to the vehicle. This was a time where she wished she would have splurged and purchased an SUV. Her little sedan would definitely not make it in snow like this.

The last time it had snowed this hard, she had been stuck at home until the roads were plowed.

"Here we are," Fin announced. He opened the door and Ward helped her to climb up into the warm truck. She shivered and settled back in the seat. They shut the door quickly and she basked in the warmth. Even the seat was heated. Her bottom was thankful for the heat that permeated through her jeans.

Skye folded her arms in front of her and tried to will her body to stop shaking. The front and driver's side windows were covered in a thick layer of snow. She peeked out the passenger window that was surprisingly clear except for some fog on the glass. She wiped it away with her hand and saw Fin and Ward outside the truck. Skye watched the two of them having a conversation. She strained to make out what they were saying, but with the noise of the heater in the pickup, she couldn't hear anything.

They were talking about her.

That was obvious.

They were friends, but she prayed that the kisses she'd shared with them wouldn't cause a rift between them. Fin had said everything was okay, and she wouldn't have to choose.

But what did that mean?

Did they want to share her?

Skye's eyes widened at the thought. Her breath caught in her throat at the image that came to mind. It was so damn hot that her heart raced.

But could she if given the opportunity?

Those kisses surfaced again.

Oh, yeah she'd be down.

They both disappeared from her sight. Within a few minutes Fin began clearing snow off the truck. Her body finally began to thaw out. The shakes and shivers were slowly disappearing. She relaxed slightly, unsure of what was going to happen next.

If someone had told her a day ago that not only would she share a kiss with Ward, but Fin as well, she would have called them crazy.

She tugged off her gloves and tucked them inside of her jacket pockets. She reached up and touched her bottom lip. It felt slightly swollen from their kisses. Thinking of how Fin had entwined his fingers with hers while Ward practically devoured her with his kiss made her press her thighs together.

His warm body had pressed against her back while Ward was in front of her—it was something she thought she could only have dreamed of.

What she wouldn't give to have that again, but next time she hoped they would be naked. A flush rippled through her at the thought.

"Shit," she breathed. Skye closed her eyes briefly and tried to shake that thought. Right now she needed to worry about getting home in this storm. She should have known better. Ward had been right to be worried. But in true Langdale native fashion, she had blown off the potential of a major storm. The weatherman was always making predictions that didn't come true.

She jumped at the sound of the driver's door opening. Fin slid into his seat and slammed the door shut. He began brushing the snow from his hair and jacket.

"It's a little frosty out there," he chuckled.

"Why don't you have a hat on?" She blurted out. Was he crazy? They lived in Illinois and it was wintertime. It was deathly cold out there. He should have had something to cover up his head. With this type of weather he'd likely catch a cold or pneumonia. He glanced over at her and grinned. His glasses were now fogged up, preventing her from seeing his eyes. He took them off and wiped them off with a small piece of cloth.

"I have one somewhere." He shrugged. He slid his glasses back on then combed his fingers through his damp hair. She felt those same butterflies she always experienced around him start to flutter to life. His smile disappeared from his face as he glanced out the windshield. "A few others out there are saying a lot of roads are already shut down. We're going to head to my house. It's not far from here. Ward is going to follow us. One of us will bring you back to get your car when the storm breaks."

Skye swallowed hard.

She thought about demanding to be taken home, but her house was across town, and there was no way that it would be possible if roads were being shut down. Going with Fin was the best option at the moment.

"Okay," she said softly. The butterflies in her stomach flapped harder. What if she had to spend the night? She suddenly felt a wave of heat overcome her. She busied herself and put her seatbelt on. Her hands were visibly shaking with the thought of what it might mean to spend the night with Fin and Ward.

Fin threw the truck in gear and slowly eased it out of the parking lot. The snow was high and it was a wonder that he was able to just drive through the drift that was in front of the vehicle. They drove in a comfortable silence as he headed toward the road.

Skye squinted and leaned forward. How the hell was he seeing anything in this blizzard? Looking at the conditions of the road, she was glad she was with him and not trying to make it home in her car. She would probably have ended up in a ditch somewhere.

Fin took his time driving down the roads and Skye gripped the door handle tight as she glanced over at him and saw him concentrating on the road. Skye just wished that Ward was with them instead of in his own truck. She sent up a quick prayer and hoped he was staying safe behind them.

"So, the kiss. Where did that come from?" The question had been burning inside her, but it felt strange to say the words out loud. But she had to know and clear the air. Skye pushed her free hand under her thigh so she wouldn't do something crazy like reach over and touch him. Fin glanced over at her for a moment before focusing back on the white-out conditions in front of them.

"I wanted to. I've been thinking about you," he admitted.

Skye's eyes widened. There had never been any signs that he was into her. He had just appeared to be friendly with everyone.

She was the awkward one when it came to interacting with him or Ward. She didn't know why she got so nervous. She'd never had this experience before she met Fin, and then Ward arrived and she was having the same reaction to him.

"But you were in a relationship with that woman," she sighed. Even if he had been thinking of her while he'd been with his ex, she would have shot him down. No way was she a homewrecker. There are plenty of men out there. She just hadn't found the right one yet, but she knew someone was out there for her.

"I was. That didn't mean I didn't like you or felt an attraction to you. Me and Lexi were complicated," he sighed. He shifted in his seat, but didn't take his eyes off the road. He slowed the truck down even further. Skye looked out her window and didn't see anything but white and shadows. This was getting worse than she expected. Were they even going in the right direction?

"I may have been with Lexi, but I still recognize a beautiful woman when I see one. Lexi and I broke up a couple months ago."

"I'm sorry."

"No need to be. It was a long time coming," Fin snorted. He glanced over at her again with a crooked grin on his lips. His gaze slid over her like a warm caress. She fought the urge to squirm in her chair. "I kept to myself. I wasn't ready to just dive right into a new relationship right away. I just needed to breathe. We'd been together for a while... but I think I'm finally ready to move on."

"Move on to what?" she asked automatically. Fin released a curse. The truck jerked and slid. Her grip on the door handle tightened. He regained control of the truck with a few expert moves.

Maybe now wasn't the best time to have this conversation.

Fin needed to stay focused to keep them on the road and fight the elements. The snow wasn't letting up at all. They were basically driving through a white out.

"You."

"Oh." Skye was stunned into silence. She hadn't really expected that as an answer. But at least she now knew Fin's intention when it came to her.

THE CHRISTMAS WONDER

Skye stood before the window and stared out into the bleak winter landscape. She couldn't see much of it, but she was watching for the headlights of Ward's truck. She couldn't believe they'd made it.

The ride from the bar to Fin's house had taken them a little over an hour and her hand had started to ache from how tightly she had held onto the door handle. But Fin had gotten them to his house safely.

They'd entered the house and, surprisingly, he still had power. It was nice and warm. She was waiting for Ward. He'd been following them, but he hadn't arrived yet. She was worried. What if he was stuck out there and needed help?

"Here you go," Fin murmured. He came to stand next to her and handed her a cup of hot cocoa. She took it and smiled. He had even put a big dollop of whip cream on top of it.

"Thank you." She took a sip and sighed. It was delicious, warm, and comforting. Just what she needed. She sighed again and turned her focus back to the window.

"Ward is fine." Fin said. He slid his arms around her and pulled her back against him. His body felt good against hers and she automatically leaned into him. She liked how it just felt so natural to be in his arms.

"How do you know? Have you spoken with him?" She took another sip of the hot chocolate. The whip cream offered a nice creamy addition to the drink. It was one of her favorites to drink on days like this.

"Yeah. I called him when I was in the kitchen. He'd spun out and gotten stuck, but he was able to get out." He must have felt her body stiffen because he tightened his hold on her and kissed her cheek. "He's okay. He'll be here soon."

"Good." She wanted both of them with her so that she could make sure they were safe and sound. She may not know what was happening between the three of them, but all she knew was that she needed Ward here with her and Fin.

"If you want to change out of those wet jeans, I think my sister-in-law and brother left some clothes from the last time they came to visit."

Skye glanced down at her jeans and grimaced. Her pant legs were soaked from the deep snow she'd had to walk through and her socks had gotten wet too.

"It would feel better to get out of these," she said. She wiggled her toes, she was pretty sure they were still frozen. Fin reached around and took the mug out of her hands.

"If you head up the stairs, the first door is the spare bedroom. There should be some clothes in the dresser you can pick from."

She nodded and turned to go, but she paused. She glanced back at him. Fin's hazel eyes were on her. With his glasses they were slightly magnified. She moved back toward him, stood on her tiptoes, and pressed her lips to his. He leaned down slightly to meet her. She stepped back and offered a small smile.

"Thanks." She spun on her heel and headed toward the staircase. She jogged up them and arrived at the second floor. She found the door to the spare room and went inside. It was a plain room with a full sized bed, and a dresser with a television resting on it.

Skye opened the dresser and looked

through the neatly folded clothes. The drawers held men and women's items. She found a few pairs of thick leggings along with clean socks.

"Thank you, sis," she murmured. She didn't know Fin's sister-in-law's name but she was thankful the woman had left a few items behind. She quickly slid her wet jeans off along with her socks and replaced them with a pair of black leggings and fluffy house socks. "That feels so good."

She wiggled her toes which immediately appreciated the warmth of the material. The sounds of a door opening and shut reached her.

Ward.

Skye scooped up her clothes and figured she'd see if she could toss them in the washing machine and wash them so they would be ready for when she was able to go home.

She paused at the door and felt a weird sensation flutter through her. She thought of her lonely little house and, honestly, did she *want* to go back there alone? She shook her head. The thoughts running through her head were crazy.

One day.

She hadn't even spent one day with Fin and Ward and she was already thinking about how much she didn't want to go home alone. She laughed shortly at her own foolishness and exited the room to head back downstairs to the men who were waiting for her.

5

Ward shook off the snow and shut the door behind him as he stepped across the threshold of Fin's house.

The roads had been a bitch to drive through.

He had been right behind Fin and Skye most of the way—at least he'd thought he had been. The snow had been coming down heavily, and prevented him from truly seeing anything beyond a foot in front of the truck.

At one point, he'd lost control of his truck and slammed into a snow drift. He was just thankful that he hadn't slid down into an unseen ditch. Even the road was unrecognizable. Thankfully there weren't many people out in that shit and he'd been able to get his truck free of the drift without too much trouble. But he was a little shaken by it.

"Took you long enough," Fin chuckled.

"Man, it wasn't that bad until I slid. Once my truck started sliding, there wasn't anything else I could do." He kicked off his boots and followed Fin into his house. He took his coat off and went over to the closet nearest them. He hung up his jacket and went into the living room. Fin's house was a nice craftsman's type home with a large fireplace as the center point of the room. His oversized couches were the perfect size for men of their height and size. But Skye was nowhere to be found.

"Glad you made it safe," Fin said, "Skye was worried about you."

There was a mug full of hot chocolate sitting on the coffee table, but no Skye. Ward had been worried about her and Fin. When he'd lost sight of them an uneasy feeling set in slightly, but Ward had to remind himself that Fin had been driving in shitty weather like this for years. He knew that his friend would make sure Skye was protected and safe.

"Where is she?" he asked.

"Upstairs changing her clothes. Her jeans and socks were soaked through," Fin said. He headed toward the kitchen and paused in the doorway. "Coffee? Or something stronger?"

"Coffee. It's cold as shit out there," Ward chuckled. Either would warm him up, but he wanted to remain sober. There was no telling how this weather was going to turn. He wanted to make sure he was of sound mind just in case they needed to go back out in the elements for whatever reason.

"Coming up." Fin disappeared from the room. Ward went over to one of the couches and took a seat. He glanced down at his jeans and grimaced. He'd changed into them before he'd left school, there was no way he'd be caught dead in gym shorts while he was out with a woman as hot as Skye. But they were soaked through because he'd had to get out and dig his truck out before he was able to get back on the road. He'd have to borrow a pair of Fin's pants. Footsteps sounded on the stairs and he turned to watch Skye as she came down the stairs from the second floor. She placed her folded pair of jeans on the bottom stairs before continuing into the room. His eyes locked on her. She had kept on the same sweater she'd worn to the bar, but now had on black leggings and a pair of thick blue socks.

"You made it," she said and a smile spread across her beautiful face. He stood as she came into the room and walked over to him. He immediately reached for her. The memory of her soft lips and the taste of her came rushing back to him.

"Did you think I wouldn't?" He smirked. He snagged her hand and brought her flush against him. He was pleased how she tilted her head back and wrapped her arms around his torso.

"I was worried," she said with a little frown. "Didn't you see what it looked like out there?"

He didn't like that she had been worried about him. He was fine. He'd been concerned about her. He reached up, cupped her face, and caressed her cheek while her warm brown eyes studied him.

"Don't ever worry about me. I was going to make it to you." He lowered his head and captured her lips with his. She opened her mouth and welcomed him. His tongue swept in and the taste of chocolate greeted him. It reminded him of her. Sweet. He was sure her other places would taste just as good. He tilted his head and deepened the kiss. His hold on her face remained, keeping her in place as he ensured she knew he had meant what he'd said.

A snowstorm wasn't going to keep him from getting to her.

He lifted his head and smiled at the expression on her face. She slowly opened her eyes and blinked as she focused on him and shook her head.

"This is crazy," she said softly.

"What is?" His thumb gently caressed her soft skin. He loved the feel of her in his arms and didn't want to let her go. He'd had his share of women, but never had this feeling or reaction to any of them before. There was something about Skye that drew him to her.

Hell, he and Fin were infatuated with

her. They had come to an agreement in that few seconds outside the truck.

If she wanted both of them, she could have them.

Ward had no problems with his friend, and this woman was enough for the both of them. He couldn't think of a better man to share this woman with. Fin was a good guy, a great friend, and would be good for Skye as much as he would.

"Well first off, that I keep kissing both of you and the two of you don't have a problem with it. Like, you're okay that I like both of you?" she asked. She reached up and removed a piece of lint from his shirt.

"Why would you think that I'd have a problem with it?" he asked.

"I don't know. Do you two normally go around sharing women?" she asked. She paused and watched him as she waited for him to answer. At that moment, he wanted to make sure that she was comfortable with him and Fin. He didn't want any doubt to be in the back of her mind about what was going on between the three of them.

"No. We've never shared a woman that we were both serious about." She didn't need to know about the few times back in college where they'd fucked the same girl. None of that had been serious. It had been about fun and everyone involved had gotten what they had needed.

"Serious?" she breathed. Her head did that cute thing she did when she was curious about something. "How do you know this is serious? We've only just met. I've known Fin for years."

"It's just a feeling," he replied, "and I'm not going to question it. I want you, Skye.". He bent his head and pressed a hard kiss to her lips. At that moment Fin re-entered the room carrying two large cups of steamy hot coffee. He released her and took the mug Fin offered him. "And so does Fin."

"Oh." She stared at both of them. She backed away and went over to the coffee table to snag her cup. She took a hefty sip. A little of the whip cream ended up on her nose. It was a cute look on her, but she must have felt it and wiped it off.

"Everything good here?" Fin arched an eyebrow.

"It is," Ward replied. "I was just telling Skye that we both want her... and that we're willing to share." Skye reached up and tucked her hair behind her ear.

"It's true, Skye. But it's your decision," Fin said. He motioned to the couch. "Why don't you have a seat so we can talk."

She nodded, a soft smile on her face, and sat down in the center of the couch. Ward slid in next to her while Fin perched on the arm on the other side of her.

She was nervous. It was obvious and Ward wanted to make her comfortable with them. This might be an awkward conversation to have, but there was no need for her to be skittish. They would respect whatever decision she made.

"Listen—" Ward began but was cut short by a loud click that echoed through the house. The room was basked in a sea of darkness and the house went completely silent. "Fuck."

The power had just gone out. This was not good. With the way the storm was raging outside, and how far the temperature had dropped, they needed to do something.

Fin stood and went over to the window.

"I can't see shit out there, but it looks like the whole street is out," Fin announced.

He turned and motioned to the fireplace. "We better get a fire started. There's no telling how long the power is going to go out."

"You still keep wood on the back porch?" Ward took a swig of the hot brew in his mug and stood. He could get the fire started so they could remain warm until the power came back on. He just hoped it was soon. This was his first winter in Langdale and it looked like the weather was trying to officially welcome him.

"Yeah. I'll run upstairs and grab a few things. Looks like we are all hunkering down here tonight," Fin said.

"What do you need me to do?" Skye asked. She sat forward and placed her mug back on the coffee table.

"If you want, there is a drawer in the kitchen near the fridge that has a flashlight and matches. If you want to snag those, that will help. I think I have candles in the hall closet next to the bathroom," Fin said.

The howling winds blew even louder outside. Ward frowned. The weather was truly showing off. Hopefully it would blow over soon. If it kept up like this, they might be trapped together for a day or two. His gaze followed Skye's shadow as she made her way out of the room.

But being trapped with a woman like Skye wasn't a bad thing at all.

"You sure do know how to build a fire," Skye chuckled. She sat on the rug near the hearth. Ward grinned back at her. They had all met back in the living room and set it up for the night. Thankfully with Ward having two large couches there would be plenty of room for them to bunker down for the night with the fireplace roaring. They had placed candles at strategic points around the room and lit them to help give them more light and the room was cozy and warm even though the rest of the house was already starting to chill. Thankfully, Fin had stored a ton of wood on the back porch that should keep them comfortable until morning.

Fin had grabbed blankets and pillows from the upstairs bedrooms and brought them down to the living room. The living room had started to look like the setting for an old fashioned slumber party. His friend had even brought down a pair of shorts for Ward to sleep in, which he appreciated.

Skye held her hands up toward the fire and sighed. Ward couldn't take his eyes off her. The light reflecting off her showcased her beauty in a way that held him captive so fiercely that he almost forgot to breathe while watching her.

Fin tipped back his mug and drained the rest of it before going back to messing with his battery powered radio. They both were on their second cup of coffee. Fin, for some reason, had a battery powered coffee percolator and made a fresh pot.

With the howling winds and the threat of the storm, it was going to be a while before Ward would feel comfortable falling asleep. Skye and her comfort were his top priority and he didn't even have to ask Fin to know that his friend felt the same.

"My father took me and my sister camping all the time. He taught me how to even make a fire without matches," Ward chuckled. "He's a survivalist who believed his children should know how to live off the land. We were always out somewhere in the wild growing up."

"Sounds fun. I've never been camping before," Skye said.

"No? How about fishing?" he asked. Fin and Ward loved to go fishing. There was nothing like getting on a boat and tossing a line out in the water and then waiting for a bite. They would have to take her. She would love it.

"Nope. Never been." She jumped from the crackling sound of wood splitting in the fire. There was a wire covering that prevented smoldering bits of wood from hopping out onto the floor, but she still seemed nervous about it.

"Skye, move back some," Fin snickered. Skye gave a sheepish smile and scooted back away from the hearth. She rolled to her knees to stand. Ward hopped up from where he was standing and moved over to her offering her a hand. The second her hand slid into his, a bolt of energy seemed to course through him from her touch. Her smile slowly disappeared as she stood up. Their eyes connected and something passed between them. He wasn't crazy, and knew there was some form of a connection between them.

Skye had filled his mind every day since he'd first met her. He tugged her close and she came without hesitation. He reached up and cupped her cheek and ever so slowly lowered his head and kissed her. She sighed, her lips parting to grant him entrance. He couldn't get enough of her taste.

He needed more.

Ward tore his mouth from hers and stared down at her. Skye's chest rose and fell hard. She opened her eyes revealing the lust in them. Ward's cock grew thick and stiff from need. He reached up and swept a finger along her bottom lip.

"Such a beauty," he murmured. Without needing to look, he was sure Fin was watching them. "Wouldn't you agree, Fin?"

"She is," Fin replied.

Skye bashfully looked away. She was so damn cute when she was shy. He tipped her chin up to force her to look him in the eye.

"I want you," Ward declared. He wasn't going to beat around the bush when it came to Skye. He wanted to make sure that she knew his intentions. He didn't mean just now for one night only. No, he wanted her as his. "And I know Fin does, too."

"The question is, can we have you tonight?" Fin asked.

He took her hand and guided her over to the couch. Fin was still propped up on the arm, his eyes locked on Skye. They stood in front of the couch. He reached up and slid a finger down along her cheek and down to her neck. Her sweater had been beckoning him to remove it. Her soft mounds were highlighted by the deep cleavage the sweater offered.

"As in together?" she asked. Her breaths were coming faster as she glanced between the two of them. His finger continued on down to the center of her chest where her lovely brown skin was exposed. Her chin tilted up slightly and an air of confidence radiated from her. He nodded when her gaze landed on him. If she wanted them together then that was what she would have.

"Say yes, Skye," Ward murmured. The only sound in the room was the crackling of the fire behind him. His cock pressed against his jeans demanding to be released. He ignored it. Skye's needs would come first before he would even think of his hard member. His finger traced along the edge of the sweater as he waited.

"Yes, to both of you," she breathed. Ward's hands dropped down to her waist. He hooked the edge of her sweater with his fingers and brought it up and over her head. Ward brought her in and captured her lips with his. He was impatient he knew, but he needed to see her naked. The fantasy of her being naked before him had kept him up many nights. Now he had her in front of him, he was going to quickly unwrap a gift that he—they— were being given tonight. "I want both of you tonight."

Ward slipped a hand behind her back and undid the clasp of her bra with one hand. Her large mounds pressed into him and drove him mad. He lifted his head and grinned.

"We're getting the best Christmas gift tonight, my friend," Ward said.

"It would seem we are," Fin said.

Ward turned her around and brought her back to him. He brushed the straps of her bra down her arms so that it could join her sweater on the floor. Her quick intake of air greeted him and he angled her so that his friend could see everything he was doing.

"Fuck, she's beautiful," Fin rasped. His focus was on Skye. Ward reached up and cupped her warm breasts, large enough to fill his hands. A moan slipped from Skye's lips as she leaned back into him. He leaned down and nuzzled her neck and breathed in her scent.

Her perfume was floral with a hint of vanilla and musk. He pressed an open mouth kiss to her throat and felt a tremor snake through her.

He played with her breasts, massaging them, cupping them, teasing the tight little buds with his fingertips. He couldn't wait to take them into his fucking mouth.

"Her pants. They need to go," Fin said. Ward smiled, only too happy to oblige his friend. Skye's whimper made his cock grow even harder. He released her breasts and allowed his hands to trail down her soft stomach. He arrived at the waistband of her leggings and paused.

"Tonight, you don't worry about a thing, Skye. We're going to take care of you."

6

Fin Milkowski was a patient man. There was not going to be any rushing tonight with Skye. His eyes were glued on Ward and Skye.

Ward was unwrapping her as if she were the most precious Christmas gift in the world.

In the candlelight, her skin practically glowed. Her large breasts had dark areolas that were tipped with pert nipples that needed to be in his mouth. Her waist was tapered, her belly had a little softness to it, but Fin didn't give a fuck about that. Her hips were wide and her thighs were thick. The only thing that remained on her body was her small scrap of panties.

"Come here, Skye," Fin rasped. He wanted to be the one to remove her last item of clothing. Her eyes opened and met his. He sat forward on the arm of the couch and couldn't tear his gaze from her. Ward dropped another kiss to her neck before allowing her to move to stand in front of Fin.

His hands trembled slightly as he reached for her. He slid his hands along her arms and up to her shoulders. He relished the feel of her buttery soft skin under his palms. Her quick intake of breath caught his attention and his hands continued on their journey and slid along her collarbone and down to her breasts. Those soft mounds made his cock ache something fierce. He lifted one and brought her closer to him to stand between his legs. He lowered his head and captured one of her nipples in his mouth. Fin's free hand rested on her waist to hold her to him while he bathed the beaded bud with his tongue and suckled hard enough to make her gasp.

Skye's fingers threaded their way through his hair and held on tight.

"Fin," she moaned. Her body swayed in place as he took his time. He trailed his tongue along her chest and arrived at the second breast and repeated the same motions with his lips and tongue.

The scent of her perfume was addicting and he inhaled while he focused on her. He hooked his finger along the edge of her panties and tugged them down. Skye lifted her legs and stepped out of them, leaving her bare for them.

Ward stepped in behind Skye. His friend had removed his clothing and was only dressed in his boxer briefs. Ward was in top shape and his torso was perfectly carved. Fin held no jealousy for his friend's figure. Ward wasn't in the worst shape but he certainly didn't have sculpted abs.

Ward's hands cupped Skye's breasts while Fin's eyes were drawn to her pussy, hidden behind a small patch of dark curls. Skye moaned again and the sound touched something deep inside of him. Ward tipped her chin up and turned her face toward him while he claimed her lips.

Fin's hands slid along her waist and hips. He wanted to memorize every facet of her delectable body. His hand moved to her center and his finger slipped through her curls and parted her slick folds.

"Fuck," he muttered. His finger met the creamy honey that poured out of her. He pushed his finger further, allowing her nectar to coat his finger. Her swollen clit greeted him. He slowly rubbed her clit, making her groan. Fin removed his fingers and brought them to his lips. Her taste exploded on his tongue. He licked every bit of her essence off. "So fucking wet, and so damn sweet."

"How could she not be? Look at her," Ward said. He pressed another hard kiss to Skye's lips. "I want a taste."

"Put her on the couch," Fin said. He stood and began unbuttoning his shirt while Ward guided Skye over and helped her onto the couch. He spread her legs open while her feet rested on the edge of the cushions, leaving her completely exposed to him. Skye's gaze held his while he began removing his clothing. His shirt got tossed somewhere on the floor and his jeans soon followed.

Ward knelt on the floor before her and chuckled.

"Look how pretty her fucking pussy is."

"Go ahead, my friend. Get a taste of her," Fin encouraged. He'd allow his friend the opportunity to go first in licking her pussy. They had all night, and Fin would get his turn to dive headfirst between her thighs soon enough.

Ward lowered his head and gave her one long lick that made Skye's back arch. She kept the eye contact with Fin as Ward tasted her, and it made his cock swell even harder. He had never had an erection this strong before. It was almost painful. He would soon need relief.

"Sweet as apple pie," Ward rasped. He returned and covered her pussy with his mouth. Fin slid off his boxers and reached for his cock. His long length was completely engorged. Skye's gaze landed on it and he stroked himself while returning back to the couch. Her breaths were coming in gasps and pants.

Her fingers threaded their way into Ward's hair. Her eyes closed briefly as a moan was torn from her lips.

"Ward," she gasped. His friend was lost

in his activity. The sounds of slurping filled the air. Fin moved to sit on the edge of the arm of the couch where he could see her and what his friend was doing to her.

"What is it, Skye? Tell me what you want." Ward lifted his head, a crooked grin on his lips. He positioned one of his fingers at her opening and pushed it inside of her.

"You," she moaned. Her gaze flickered to him before coming back to Fin. "And you. I want both of you."

Skye's head fell back against the pillows. Ward slowly thrust his finger in and out of her. Skye's hips gyrated against Ward's hand as he slowly fucked her with the single digit.

"You'll have both of us," Fin replied. He tightened his hold on his cock. Droplets formed at the head of his cock and he swept his thumb over the head of his cock and used those droplets as lubricant for his strokes. He couldn't wait to feel her slick channel gripping him.

Patience.

In due time, he'd be deep inside of her.

"Any way you want us," Ward added in. He withdrew his one finger then pushed two inside her. Fin knew what his friend was doing. They would have to ensure she was prepared for them. Both of them were big men, and she was going to have to stretch to fit them. Fin never would want to cause her pain, and he was sure Ward felt the same. "She's so fucking tight. Are you seeing this?"

"I am," Fin said. He watched Ward sink his two fingers deep inside of her. When he pulled them back they were coated with her cream. Fin continued to stroke his cock as he watched his friend.

Fin hadn't known for sure how the night was going to go. When he'd gone upstairs and grabbed blankets and pillows, he had grabbed something else he'd figured they might need. He'd stashed the tube in the drawer of the table by the couch. If they hadn't ended up here, then she wouldn't have known about what he'd hid. It would come in handy, very soon.

Ward's head lowered and he latched on to her swollen clit while he continued to fuck her with his fingers. Skye's moans were growing louder. Fin reached over and took her chin in his hand and turned her to face him. Her wide brown eyes were filled with lust and Fin's gaze dropped down to her plump lips.

Lips that needed to be wrapped around him.

"Open your mouth, Skye," He ordered. He positioned himself closer to her and guided the head of his cock to her mouth. She held his gaze as she wrapped those fucking perfect lips around the head of his thick cock. He bit back a curse and moved his hand to the top of her head. He held her in place while he pushed forward gently sending more of his length inside of her mouth. She opened wider to accommodate his thick girth. "That's a good girl."

She moaned, sending vibrations along this cock. Fin bit back a curse. He withdrew slightly and began a slow steady rhythm. She reached up with one hand to hold on to his cock. He couldn't fit his entire length into her mouth and throat without hurting her, but her hands slid along his length as he moved. Her strokes were steady, and went the full length of him where her mouth couldn't reach.

Ward's head remained buried in between her legs as he continued to feast on her. His hands were increasing their pace, as he fucked her faster with his fingers. Her head moved along with his motions. She closed her eyes and continued to suck Fin's cock perfectly. Her saliva slid along his length and her grip on his cock created the best fucking sensation in the world.

Her chest rose and fell swiftly and her muffled moans filled the air. Then she released his cock from her mouth as her head fell back. Her body trembled while a scream was ripped from her lips. It was a beautiful sight to watch her climax. Skye's hand kept stroking him as she fell into the waves of her orgasm. Fin could feel he was close and wasn't going to last long. His hand joined hers, sliding along his cock, and a familiar sensation coursed through his body. He wasn't going to be able to hold back.

He pulled her head toward him.

"Open. Now," he demanded. Skye's eyes snapped open and landed on his cock. She didn't hesitate to do as he commanded. He leaned forward just as his release spewed from his cock and into her mouth. She kept her mouth open and allowed him to stroke himself and cover her tongue with his release. She swallowed and leaned forward and sucked his cock into her mouth. She stroked his cock and sucked hard as if to milk more from him. This little woman was greedy, and if she needed more, they would both give her what she needed.

Fin groaned loudly as his body shook. She was going to suck his fucking soul out of him, and he'd let her have it. He pushed forward as far as he could go and she didn't even complain. She took his fucking cock down her throat like a woman on a mission.

"Swallow everything he gives you," Ward encouraged her. She nodded confirming she'd heard him. He raised up on his knees and planted kisses along her neck and chest. His hand was still between her legs with his fingers inside of her. He withdrew his fingers from her and began licking them clean. "So damn good. How did we get so lucky?"

Fin didn't know. He moved his hand from the top of her head and pulled his cock from her mouth. He fought to catch his breath. Her mouth was so fucking dangerous. His cock was still swollen, and throbbed with the aftermath of his release. She was fucking beautiful.

The sight of some of his release and her saliva rested on her lips and chin made his cock start to grow hard again.

7

Skye's breaths were coming hard and fast. She couldn't believe she was not only here with Ward and Fin, but they were both going to fuck her.

Skye licked her lips.

The taste of Fin's release was still on her tongue. He reached out and swept his thumb across her bottom lip.

"Good girl," Fin said. He reached up and removed his glass and placed them on the table next to the couch. He jerked his head toward the couch. "Ward on the couch."

Ward released her breast and glanced up at her. He leaned forward and covered her mouth with his. She moaned and wrapped her arms around his neck. She couldn't get enough of these two. Ward's tongue and fingers were amazing. She hadn't had a hard orgasm like that before. She'd had mediocre ones with her vibrators and dildos and an occasional one with a past lover, but nothing as earth shattering as this one.

But then again, she'd never had one man eating her pussy while she sucked another man's cock before. This was something she could definitely get used to. Her body was on fire and her nipples were drawn into tight little buds. Her pussy was soaked, and her clit was swollen. Ward had ensured he'd paid enough attention to it. There was no doubt that man knew what he was doing.

Ward released her nipple and stood. He slid down his shorts and Skye swallowed hard. Not only was Fin thick and long, Ward was too. They were wondering how they had gotten lucky with her, it should be her thanking the good Lord above for giving her two men who were blessed in the dick department. Ward moved and took a seat next to her.

Skye didn't hesitate to throw a leg over him and straddle him. Tonight was not the time for her to be shy. She was going to be selfish and take what she wanted and what she had needed. She had asked Santa for a man under her tree, but it would seem two days before Christmas, she was getting two of them.

Her pussy pulsed with the thought of sliding down onto Ward's thick dick. His length was nestled in between her legs. She rotated her hips and slid along the length of him.

"Oh, god," she moaned. Her core clenched with need. She wanted to feel him stretch her out as she knew he would. With a monster cock like his, she was going to have to work to take him. Ward's hands rested on her ass and helped her slide along him.

"Take what you need," Ward murmured. His gaze was laser focused on her.

She felt beautiful.

Sexy.

Wanted.

These two men made her feel like she was the only woman in the world. The storm raged on outside, but she could care less. All that mattered was what was happening between the three of them.

"I need you inside me," she breathed. She held onto the cushions behind his head.

"Then lift up." Ward helped her up then reached underneath her to grab his cock. He nestled the broad tip of it against her entrance and she gasped and widened her legs above him before she began to sink down on him. She cried out from the invasion of such a thick girth, paused, lifted up slightly and then began to lower herself onto his cock.

"Fuck," she muttered.

She closed her eyes and tried to get herself to relax more.

She was determined to take him fully inside of her. Her nails dug into the pillows as she finally sank all the way onto his cock. Tears stung her lashes and. She blinked them away and smiled at her accomplishment.

"Skye, baby. You're so fucking tight," Ward rasped. He closed his eyes and rested his head back on the couch cushions. She wiggled a little then moved slightly. Fin stood from where he'd been perched and went to table by the couch. He pulled something out of the drawer then moved behind her. She turned her focus back to riding

Ward's cock. His hands were tight on her ass as he helped guide her up and down his length.

A cry escaped her as he thrust his hips up sending his dick deep inside her. She leaned down and kissed him and one of his hands came to rest on the back of her head and held her in place as he fucked her mouth his tongue. She returned the kiss with the same heat and fever.

She moaned from the sensations coursing through her body as her pussy took a pounding from his hard strokes. Fin's hand fell onto her shoulder and she tore her lips from Ward's and looked over her shoulder at him.

"Lean over more," he commanded. She didn't know when he'd become so damn dominant and bossy, but Skye loved it. A shudder went up her spine as she paused her motions, leaving Ward buried inside of her pussy. She leaned raised up a little and leaned forward, and her pussy clenched around Ward's cock, making him groan and curse.

Her eyes widened at the feeling of his finger rubbing something cool along the rim of her asshole. She'd never had anyone she felt was worthy of gifting that hole to before.

However, tonight Ward and Fin could put their dicks wherever they wanted.

She inhaled sharply as he pushed finger into her tight hole. She moaned and her pussy pulsated around Ward's thick cock. She closed her eyes briefly, loving the feeling of Fin's finger as it moved deep inside her forbidden entrance.

"You like that, huh?" Ward asked. His gray eyes watched her as she remained still. Fin's finger withdrew slightly then he pushed two inside her puckered rim. A moan tore from her as she felt more of the cool gel coat her opening.

"God, yes," she whimpered. Who the hell was this brazen hussy? But she hoped this woman stayed around. Skye, who was normally shy and clumsy around these two, was finding that all of that had gone out the window. "I need more. Fin, please. Put your cock in my ass."

Again, who was this woman?

She didn't know, but all Skye knew was that she wanted Fin and Ward to fuck her at the same time. She needed to have their cocks inside of her. If she were to die tonight, she'd be one happy woman.

"The lady has spoken, my friend," Ward said.

"Don't worry, Skye. I'm about to," Fin rasped.

Ward's hands spread her cheeks wide for Fin. Ward's cock was already buried in her pussy, and he was opening her wide so his friend could slide his cock into her ass. Apparently, that was what true friends were for.

Skye's breath caught in her throat at the feeling of Fin's cock pushing at her anal rim. She exhaled sharply as he pushed forward, introducing the thick head of his cock into her tight hole. Her muscles gave some resistance, but Fin pushed farther inside. He paused and leaned over and sprinkled her shoulder and back with kisses. There was a slight burning sensation, but it was slowly dissipating.

"Relax, baby. It's going to feel good." Fin's warm breath skated along her shoulder and she nodded, unable to speak. He pushed in more and she could have cried. She had never felt so damn full before. One cock already had her full, but two of them was heaven. She couldn't ask for anything better.

Fin continued pressing forward until he was fully sheathed inside her ass. She gripped the couch pillows tight in her hand. Her eyes fluttered closed while she focused on breathing. She was determined to have them both, and right now she had succeeded.

Now they needed to fuck her.

As if reading her mind, Ward thrust upward into her pussy. She gasped from the move. Fin withdrew slightly and then sank back inside her ass. A cry tore from her throat as they both began to move in a steady rhythm. She could do nothing but hold still as the two men fucked her.

Fin's hand came up and gripped her hair and held her in place as he moved behind her. Ward's hands were on her waist, holding her steady as he thrust deeper inside of her. Skye basked in the feeling of two cocks penetrating her at the same time. This was the closest thing to Heaven she had ever experienced.

They increased their pace and Skye's

cries filled the air along with the sound of their skin slapping against each other. Ward's cock was positioned perfectly, hitting her sensitive spots at just the right angle. She pushed her hand between her legs to rub her clit and her heart raced from the sensations coursing through her body. Nothing but pleasure filled her.

"Skye," Ward groaned. His grip on her hips tightened. Fin's fingers in her hair held her in place as he thrust harder into her ass. Skye's body began to tremble and shake as she teetered on the edge of her second orgasm. She'd never thought she'd be a multi-orgasm woman. Apparently she hadn't had the right partner—partners—to help get her there.

Ward and Fin were steady in their conquest to fuck her to oblivion, and they were succeeding. Her muscles tightened and soon she was tumbling head first into another orgasm. She screamed as her body shook from the electrical current that raced through her.

"Fuck. Skye," Ward shouted. Skye's voice grew hoarse as she rode the waves of her climax. Ward's body trembled underneath hers and his nails dug into her hips. A warmth began to fill her and he thrust harder, filling her with his seed as he came.

Fin's groans were mixed in with theirs. He roared behind her as he began to fill her ass with his cum. She held still as they both thrust and sent their release deep within her.

"Fill me up," she moaned greedily as she welcomed their seed. "Give me all your cum"

It gave her a funny feeling inside of her chest knowing that she had pleased both of these men. Skye wasn't sure how long they remained there, but she wanted to ensure they both had finished coming. Fin was the first to move. He withdrew from her and she immediately missed the feeling of fullness and the stretch of his cock in her ass. He fell onto the couch next to Ward. In the low light, she took notice of the fine sheen of sweat on them all. She smiled and didn't feel ashamed about what had occurred.

"Baby. Lift up and go to Fin," Ward said. He withdrew from her and it was then she felt the dribble from his and Fin's release running out of her onto her ass and thighs.

Fin positioned himself in the corner of the couch and opened his arms. She tossed a leg over Ward and went to Fin. She held back a wince from the slight pain she felt. It was a wonder she was even able to move after having their monster cocks in her at the same time. She went over to Fin and went into his arms. He pulled her halfway to lay on the couch with him where she was spooned in front of him with his chest to her back. She rested her head on his arm and sighed.

Ward stood and disappeared out of the room. She frowned. *Where was he going?*

"We didn't hurt you, did we?" Fin asked.

"No, not at all," Skye said. His hand slid down her stomach and parted her legs. She inhaled sharply as he brought the wetness that was collected there and started smearing it along her stomach.

"What are you doing?" she giggled. He leaned in and kissed the side of her neck. She moaned and tilted her head to give him better access. His fingers returned between her legs and repeated the motion.

"You look so sexy with our cum on you," he breathed. He nipped her neck then soothed it with his tongue. "When I pulled my cock out of you, all I could see was my cum sliding out of your ass. It was such a pretty sight to see."

His finger began to draw little circles on her clit and Skye moaned. The swollen bud was so damn sensitive and here he was playing with it. A shiver rippled through her. How the hell was she getting turned on again?

"You want to put it back in there?" she asked. Just thinking of how he had felt pushing inside of her had her ready to bend over for him again. She closed her eyes and basked in the warmth of him. The fire was dying down, but that didn't matter. Skye's body was close to detonating. With what had occurred between the three of them, she was surprised they hadn't set the damn house on fire.

"Soon. The next time I come in you, it will be in your pussy." Skye's breath caught in her throat. Fin's tongue slid along her neck while he trailed his hand up her stomach and captured her breasts. She leaned back into him. She didn't care what she looked like, she just knew she was becoming addicted to the pleasure these two men gave her. "I want to see my cum drip out of your pretty pink pussy."

A whimper escaped her at the thought. She closed her eyes and wanted that too. She wanted him and Ward to fill her with all of their release.

After tonight, she didn't think she would ever want to let them go.

Was it too soon to be thinking of a future?

She didn't know, but it would be something they would be speaking about.

She wanted both of them.

Ward returned to the room and walked over to the couch. He knelt down before her and motioned to her legs.

"Let me clean you up," he said. She smiled softly as she felt a warm wet cloth slide along her thighs. She'd never had a lover—much less two at the same time—who wanted to ensure she was well taken care of. He carefully wiped her clean with the wash cloth before tossing it onto the floor. He snagged one of the blankets and covered her and Fin up. He leaned over and pressed a chaste kiss to her lips. "Rest for now."

She nodded and snuggled down in Fin's arms. Her eyes drifted over to the window. It was pitch dark outside and with the howling of the wind, she felt at peace. This Christmas was turning out better than she could have imagined. Santa was showing off. He'd made her wait and then he'd showed up and showed out by bringing her two sexy men who wanted no one but her.

Skye smiled as she laid her head against Fin's chest. She'd rest for now, but soon, she would need her men again.

EPILOGUE
ONE YEAR LATER

Skye flew around the kitchen in a wicked rush. Christmas fell on a Tuesday this year and with the holiday vacations giving them all time off, Fin, Ward and Skye were going to take advantage of their days off.

Skye's favorite time of the year was upon them, and she had woken up early so she could cook breakfast for the three of them. It wouldn't be anything fancy; she still had to finish off her holiday cooking. She had tossed on her robe and matching slippers and dashed down to the kitchen. After breakfast and gift opening, she'd throw on some proper clothes and get to work on their holiday meal.

She stood before the oven waiting for the last minute before the timer sounded.

It had been one magical year and she had fallen in love with her two men. She couldn't even begin to think of what her life would be like without them. She smiled and remembered how this time last year she had spent a magical weekend snowed in with Fin and Ward.

Now they were living together. They had recently moved into an older home that had previously been utilized as an inn. The innkeepers had been looking to retire and move to a warmer climate. The three of them had purchased the big old house with no plans to open it as a business. Instead, they had renovated it and turned it into a beautiful spacious home for the three of them to live in. Each of them had their own private suites, and it couldn't have worked out better.

Ward and Fin shared her completely. Some nights just one of them would stay with her in her suite while other nights they came to her together. Skye was blessed to have two men who were dedicated to her and attentive to her needs.

THE CHRISTMAS WONDER

She couldn't ask for a better life.

When she had first explained to her family that she loved Fin and Ward and that they were going to make a life together, they had been taken by surprise... but only at first. Once her parents had met the guys, they cast aside their doubts. They were happy with how much the men loved their daughter and that was all that mattered to her.

The timer on the stove sounded and she hit the button to turn it off. The kitchen was her domain. With how much she loved cooking and baking, Fin and Ward had ensured she had the kitchen of her dreams. She pulled out the biscuits she had made from scratch and spun around to place the baking pan on a cooling rack.

She felt a little giddy as she set up breakfast because she had hidden a special gift underneath the tree. It was a miracle Ward hadn't found it. Last night, they had stayed up late wrapping gifts for his family members and hers. She had tucked his and Fin's special gift underneath the tree in the back.

"How did I know I would find you here?" Ward's voice echoed from the doorway. She glanced over and felt her heart skip a beat. His blond hair stood up on end as if he'd only used his fingers to comb it. He was dressed in gray basketball shorts and a navy blue t-shirt. She smiled and reached up to push her braids out of her face. She had recently had her hair braided and loved the style since it allowed her more freedom. She didn't have to worry about flat ironing her hair or styling it because the braids were so easy to manage.

"Maybe you smelled the aroma of bacon floating through the air?" She shrugged. It wasn't that they didn't cook, but it was more than likely that it would be her in the kitchen than Fin. A small smile curved her lips as Ward pushed off the doorway and made his way to her. His intense stare made the butterflies in her stomach churn the way they always did. It didn't matter how long they had been together, she still got that same feeling when around him. He stopped in front of her and tugged her to him. She went willingly and wrapped her arms around his waist. "Merry Christmas."

"Merry Christmas." He tipped her chin

up toward him and took her lips in a soft and slow kiss. Skye pressed close to him, loving the feeling of his hard body against hers. He pulled away slightly and studied her. He reached up and caressed the side of her face. "You didn't have to get up and cook us breakfast."

"I wanted to," Skye admitted. She glanced at the stove and felt satisfied. She hadn't gotten too carried away. Feeding two grown men with healthy appetites was quite a challenge. There were only three of them living in the house, but she had to cook as if ten people lived with her. Today, she'd kept it quite simple. Homemade biscuits, grits, eggs and bacon. That should keep them satisfied until dinner was ready.

"Merry Christmas." Fin strolled into the kitchen. He was dressed in his red pajama pants with the matching top she'd found him. She grinned at him as he made his way over to her. She slipped from Ward's hold and went into Fin's arms.

"Morning, sunshine," she said. She stood up on her tiptoes for her morning kiss from him. Her heart raced at the feeling of his lips pressed against hers. She was one lucky girl, and she knew it. She pulled back and patted him on his chest. "Before we eat breakfast, I want to give you two a gift."

"It can't wait until after we eat?" Fin's eyes strayed over to the stove. She laughed and took him by the hand and then reached for Ward's hand and entwined his fingers with hers.

"This won't take long. Now that it's Christmas I can't wait any longer," she giggled. She tugged them behind her as she made her way out of the kitchen.

"Hurry up. I'm hungry," Fin chuckled. She snickered and glanced up at him. He was the most impatient of the two. Her heart skipped a beat thinking of what she had waiting for them. When they got to the living room, motioned for them to take a seat on the couch then beelined it to the tree and picked up the rectangular box she had wrapped for them.

It was silly to do this, but she wanted to make it special.

She turned around and walked back to them. Her core clenched at the sight of the two men she loved more than life sitting on the couch. She stopped in front of them, knelt on the floor, and put the box in between them on the couch.

"Merry Christmas, my loves," she murmured. Her heart pounded in her chest as she watched them. They were the best of friends and did everything together. They had taken her on multiple camping and fishing trips, and they were even teaching her how to scuba dive so she would be able to participate the next time they went on a trip.

She was in love with these two and so thankful that her wish had finally been answered. It was a wonder that not only had she found one love of her life, but two.

"What is this?" Fin muttered. They worked to get the box open. It was a little big for the gift that was nestled inside, but it was all she had. They lifted the top and moved the tissue paper. "Seriously what is this?"

"Holy shit." Ward's eyes went wide. He reached inside and pulled out their gift. It was her ultrasound photo. He jerked around to look at her. "You're pregnant?"

Fin's quick intake of breath filled the air.

He took the photo from Ward and studied it.

"I am," she sniffed. Her heart was pounding and she was sure it would soon burst out of her chest. Ward jumped up, scooped her up into his arms, and swung her around. She laughed and held on tight. This secret had been so hard to keep. She hadn't been paying close attention to her cycle. Welp, she'd missed three of them. They had knocked her up.

"I love you so much." Ward pressed a hard kiss to her lips and set her down on the floor. She turned and found Fin standing next to them with a wide grin on his face.

"Is *that* why you were sneaking around?" Fin said. He pulled her to him and wrapped his arms around her. She basked in the feeling of him and nuzzled her face against his chest. She tipped her head back and smiled. It would figure that Fin would be the one to pick up on her trying to hide something from them.

"I was not sneaking," she protested. "I was being *very* careful to not let the cat out of the bag. I wanted to surprise you two."

"Consider us surprised," Fin said incredulously. "I love you, Skye and this baby is the best gift you could give us.". He leaned down and placed one hell of a kiss on her.

Skye was filled with so much love and happiness. This had to be the best Christmas a girl could ask for. She had the loves of her life with her, and she was pregnant. She pulled back, having realized something.

"You didn't look at the photo close enough," she said.

"What do you mean?" Ward said. She chuckled and shook her head. She took them both by the hand and pulled them close to her. They immediately encircled her, giving her an immediate feeling of safety and love.

"There are two babies in that picture. We're having twins."

The shocked expressions on Fin and Ward faces caused Skye to fall into a fit of laughter. She brought the two loves of her life close and hugged them both. They would be fine once the initial shock wore off. Skye couldn't believe how lucky she was. Their house would be full of love and happiness.

Her face hurt from smiling so much. Here she had thought Santa had been ignoring her wishes. It would appear that Santa had been paying attention to her list after all. He had just waited for the right moment to deliver.

A NOTE FROM THE AUTHOR

Dear reader,

Thank you for reading The Christmas Wonder. It felt good to be back in our little snowy town of Langdale! Mother Nature sure does not like this town, but that's okay...love will be found.

I hope you enjoyed Skye, Fin and Ward's story. I had a blast writing their story and too bad I had to keep it short since this is a novella series. I certainly could have kept going with these three. But that's okay...they got their happy ending!

Please don't forget to leave a review for this book once you are done reading!

Happy reading,
Peyton Banks

THE CHRISTMAS SECRET

There's no place like home for the holidays...

When her best friend comes home for the holidays, there is something different about him. Gracie Logan had been best friends with Harris since they were in junior high. Growing up, he had been the popular guy in town who all the women swooned over.

And she had been stuck in the friend category forever.

Keeping her lips sealed about her crush, she decided to continue being the one thing he needed most—a friend.

Harris Bates was home for the holidays.

One look at Gracie and knew he could no longer fight what he had known for years.

She was the one for him.

Sparks began to fly, and they can't ignore the intense attraction between them. Will they act on what is brewing between them? One thing they both knew was that nothing will ever be the same again.

The Christmas Secret is a steamy, holiday BWWM romance. For readers who love sexy, friends to lovers romance, this is for you. This short novella is reserved for mature readers only.

Available now!

ABOUT THE AUTHOR

USA TODAY bestselling author, Peyton Banks, is the alter ego of a city girl who is a romantic at heart. Her mornings consist of coffee and daydreaming up the next steamy romance book ideas. She loves spinning romantic tales of hot alpha males and the women they love. Make sure you check her out!

Sign up for Peyton's Newsletter to find out the latest releases, giveaways and news! Visit www.peytonbanks.com/newsletter to sign up!

Want to know the latest about Peyton Banks? Follow her online:

ALSO BY PEYTON BANKS

<u>Current Free Short Story</u>
Summer Escape

<u>A Langdale Christmas</u>
The Christmas Secret
The Christmas Wish
The Christmas Gift
The Christmas Wonder

<u>Book Boyfriend Dating Agency</u>
Surgeon Book Boyfriend

<u>Silver Creek Ranch (Shared World)</u>
Wrangling Her Cowboy

<u>Lunchtime Chronicles (Peyton's)</u>
Polish Boy
Thick & Beefy
Rich & Decadent

<u>The Keith Brothers</u>

Mr. Hotness

Mr. Arrogant

<u>Blazing Eagle Ranch Series</u>

Back in the Saddle

Knockin' the Boots

Roping a Cowboy

Country at Heart

Cowboy, Take Me Away

Hard to Forget

<u>Special Weapons & Tactics Series</u>

Dirty Tactics (Special Weapons & Tactics 1)

Dirty Ballistics (Special Weapons & Tactics 2)

Dirty Operations (Special Weapons & Tactics 3)

Dirty Alliance (Special Weapons & Tactics 4)

Dirty Justice (Special Weapons & Tactics 5)

Dirty Trust (Special Weapons & Tactics 6)

Dirty Secrets (Special Weapons & Tactics 7)

Dirty Ultimatum (Special Weapons & Tactics 8)

<u>SWAT boxset, books 1-3</u>

<u>Trust & Honor Series (BWWM)</u>

Dallas

Dalton

Interracial Romances (BWWM)

Pieces of Me

Hard Love

Retain Me

Silent Deception

African American Romance

Breaking The Rules

Mafia Romance

Unexpected Allies (The Tokhan Bratva 1)

Milton Keynes UK
Ingram Content Group UK Ltd.
UKHW031445291124
451807UK00005B/331

9 798330 575480